GRADUATING PRESENT

The Vietnam War & The Class of '66

EDMUND SHELBY

Graduating Present:
The Vietnam War & The Class of '66

EDMUND SHELBY

© 2022

ALL RIGHTS RESERVED.

NONFICTION

ISBN 978-1-934894-80-4

BOOK DESIGN & COVER CONCEPT : EK SCOUT LARKEN
FRONT COVER IMAGE : JESSIE LYNNE KELTNER
BACK COVER IMAGE : LAURA CHOUETTE (UNSPLASH)
AUTHOR HEADSHOT : EYE SCOUT IMAGES
INSIDE PHOTOS : COLLECTION OF THE AUTHOR

*Printed and bound in the United States of America.
Protected by the First Amendment of the U.S. Constitution.*

No part of this publication may be reproduced, stored in a retrieval system or transmited in any form or by any means—electronic, mechanical, photocopying, recording or otherwise—without prior written permision of the author, except for brief quotations referenced in reviews or scholarly work.

Published in Kentucky

INDIE EDITORIAL & DESIGN CONSULTING

★

GRADUATING PRESENT

The Vietnam War & The Class of '66

*Thank you, Anne,
for 50 years of love and support.*

INTRODUCTION

Sugar, Sugar?

Boys & Girls No Longer

According to Billboard magazine, "Sugar, Sugar" by The Archies was the number one pop song in America on September 21, 1969.

Matt Stewart was killed in Vietnam's Quang Ngai Province on that very day. Six days short of his 21st birthday, Matt was the only member of the Corbin (Kentucky) High School Class of 1966 to die in that war ... but he was not the only one affected.

Nearly all members of the class had been born in 1948. There were 48 boys, and over one third of them served in the military. Some of them went to Vietnam, some elsewhere in the world. They came back, no longer boys, having learned that life isn't sugar, sugar.

Many of the girls in the class also learned that life isn't so sweet. No longer candy girls, some married men who returned from war with PTSD and the effects of Agent Orange. Some worked with veterans in VA hospitals.

The Class of '66, whether they served or not, came to accept that adjusting to the personal and cultural residue of their generation's war wasn't ever a choice. It was just something that had to be done.

Class of '66 ~ Corbin High School ~ Corbin, Kentucky

CHAPTER ONE

What Forces Shaped Us?

Observing Origins: Flipping Through the '50s

Most of the Class of '66 were born in **1948**, just after the end of World War II. One of the most popular songs that year was "I'm Looking Over a Four Leaf Clover" by Art Mooney and his Orchestra. A major news story was the Soviet blockade of Berlin and the American flights to supply the city. This was one of the most dramatic conflicts in the Cold War that would haunt those students until well into their adult lives.

Vietnam would become a hot part of that cold war.

←--→

In the **1940s**, President Harry Truman had set the stage for what the Class of '66 would eventually have to deal with: he decided to support the French, who wanted to reclaim the colony in southeast Asia that they had held before World War II. Ho Chi Minh, the leader in the northern part of Vietnam, had admired the U.S. and had tried to get America to support his effort to create an independent country. Though the French had been heavily supported by the U.S., Vietnamese forces defeated the French at Dien Bien Phu, thus ending France's attempt to reclaim its former colony.

Truman, though, saw the threat of Communism, and Ho's part in that movement, as something no American supporter of Capitalism could allow.

Max Hastings, in his *Vietnam, An Epic Tragedy, 1945-1975*, notes, "… as France's will to fight weakened, that of the U.S. stiffened; the colonial army became increasingly an American proxy. Truman and [Secretary of State Dean] Acheson, far from pressing Paris to negotiate with the Viet Minh, urged it to do no such thing. Here was Washington's first big blunder in Indochina, from which U.S. policy-making never recovered."

←--→

When Dwight Eisenhower took over as President in January **1953**, he saw the Communists as our major threat in the world, and continued supporting the French.

After the debacle at Dien Bien Phu, an international agreement had been reached that split Vietnam into two sections, North and South, with the promise of nationwide elections in 1956.

The wheels of a different path to destiny, however, were already in motion. Looking back through the long lens of history, it's easy to see that the people in the nascent Class of '66 were headed eventually for a full, face-on conflict in an unknown and far away place called Vietnam.

←--→

The Class of '66 entered First Grade in **1954**, a year that witnessed rock-and-roll music making the scene with "Rock Around the Clock" by Bill Haley and the Comets.

Television had taken off in the 1950s. As children, the Class of '66 regularly viewed characters such as Hopalong Cassidy, The Cisco Kid, and Howdy Doody. They also witnessed how news reporting changed because of this innovative technology.

In 1954, Congress passed the Communist Control Act that outlawed the Communist Party in the United States. This was also the year the U.S. watched Senator Joseph McCarthy and his controversial political crusade known as "McCarthyism" emerge with the Senate's Army-McCarthy Hearings—a smear campaign that defamed American citizens and ruined many careers.

Max Hastings reports that in 1954 Secretary of State John Foster Dulles "told congressional leaders that the U.S. would adopt a new policy to defend southern Vietnam, Laos and Cambodia from Communist takeovers, to 'hold this area and fight subversion with all the strength we have.'"

U.S. aid to South Vietnam, according to Hastings, went from $1 million in 1954 to $322 million the following year.

←--→

In **1955**, when the Corbin kids were in second grade, an African-American teenager named Emmett Till was brutally murdered in Mississippi in a racist attack, making him a posthumous icon of the Civil Rights Movement. Claudette Colvin, an African-American teenaged girl, was arrested for refusing to give up her seat on a Montgomery, Alabama, bus. A few months later, activist Rosa Parks would likewise hold her own seat on a city bus, thus setting in motion a prolonged boycott that would change U.S. history.

Musically that year, Little Richard recorded "Tutti Frutti." Elvis Presley and Bo Diddley appeared on TV for the first time.

Captain Kangaroo debuted on television, and Mary Martin's stage portrayal of *Peter Pan* was broadcast for the first time. Kermit the Frog was "born." *Alfred Hitchcock Presents, The Mickey Mouse Club*, and *Gunsmoke* premiered on TV.

The Salk polio vaccine received full FDA approval, and American cytogeneticist Joe Hin Tjio discovered the correct number of human chromosomes: 46.

The first edition of the *Guinness Book of Records* was published in 1955. Both Disneyland and the original McDonald's restaurant opened. Actor James Dean died in a car crash; his film *Rebel Without a Cause* was released a month later.

Militarily in 1955, *USS Nautilus*, the first nuclear-powered submarine, put to sea for the first time. The prototype Lockheed *U-2* reconnaissance aircraft made its first flight. And the Pentagon announced a plan to develop intercontinental ballistic missiles (ICBMs), armed with nuclear weapons.

In world events, Winston Churchill resigned as Prime Minister of the United Kingdom at age 80, due to ill health.

West Germany became a sovereign nation. Ngo Dinh Diem proclaimed Vietnam to be a republic, with himself as its president.

November 1, 1955, marked the official start date of the Vietnam War between the Democratic Republic of Vietnam and Republic of Vietnam; the North was allied with the Viet Cong.

←---→

And so came **1956**, when the U.S. "...assumed full responsibility for training and equipping the [South] Vietnamese Army and established a Military Assistance and Advisory Group (MAAG) in Saigon," according to H.R. McMaster in his book *Dereliction Of Duty: Lyndon Johnson, Robert McNamara, the Joint Chiefs of Staff, and the Lies that Led to Vietnam*.

Thanks to their black-and-white TV screens, the Corbin kids witnessed a grandfatherly Eisenhower win re-election in 1956. They may also have seen images of Soviet tanks rolling into the streets of Budapest, Hungary.

They knew the world was dangerous.

After all, there were duck-and-cover drills in school, just in case the "eight-foot tall, atheist Russians" should send nuclear destruction on every little American town.

But the nation's fears were also distracted by Elvis Presley, who had five songs in the top 15 of *Billboard's* hits in 1956—"Heartbreak Hotel," "Don't Be Cruel," "Hound Dog," "I Want You, I Need You, I Love You," and "Love Me Tender." Things were fun; things were good. Prosperity in America was in full swing.

Those future members of the Class of '66 were too young to notice that the promised elections in Vietnam did not occur. The leadership in South Vietnam did not want a vote, because they feared they would lose. The U.S. had already made up its mind not to see South Vietnam lost.

←---→

In **1957** the Soviet Union launched the world's first artificial satellite, Sputnik 1. This started what became known as the Space Race. It also raised concern in the U.S. that if the Soviets could build and launch Sputnik, they could send nuclear-tipped missiles to America.

The Class of '66, who were still children in the mid-1950s, knew all about Sputnik, but they were just as fascinated by *The Woody Woodpecker Show* and *Leave It To Beaver*, two of the most popular television shows that year. And on radio, they heard the year's top two popular songs: "All Shook Up" by Elvis Presley and Pat Boone's "Love Letters In The Sand."

Stanley Karnow, in his seminal work *Vietnam: A History,* wrote, "As early as October 1957, on instructions from Hanoi, the Communists in the South organized thirty-seven armed companies, most of them in the impenetrable forests and marshes of the western fringe of the Mekong Delta."

The makings of guerrilla war were in place.

←---→

Two of the top movies in **1958** were *Vertigo* and *Cat on a Hot Tin Roof*. Brothers from Kentucky hit the pop charts with "All I Have To Do Is Dream" and the flip side "Claudette." The Everly Brothers also scored with "Bird Dog" and "Devoted To You."

Scandal hit the television industry when accusations surfaced that popular quiz shows were rigged.

Also in pop culture that year, the hula hoop was first marketed in the U.S., and Elvis Presley was inducted into the U.S. Army.

Top Westerns on television were *Gunsmoke, Wagon Train, Have Gun Will Travel,* and *The Rifleman.*

In world events, Egypt and Syria united to form the United Arab Republic, Fidel Castro's revolutionary army began its attacks on Havana, and the U.S. began nuclear tests over the South Atlantic.

In Kentucky, one of the worst school bus accidents in U.S. history occurred near Prestonsburg; 27 people were killed.

As the class ended fifth grade and entered sixth, Alaska and Hawaii became the 49th and 50th states in **1959**. America's first astronauts were selected. Fidel Castro came to power in Cuba. Vice-President Richard Nixon and Soviet Premier Nikita Kruschev argued about the advantages of Capitalism and Communism in a "model kitchen" display at the American National Exhibition in Moscow. Their conversation became known as the Kitchen Debate.

Culturally that year, *Rawhide, The Twilight Zone,* and *Bonanza* were popular television shows, and the Barbie doll was introduced. The two top songs of 1959 were Johnny Horton's "The Battle of New Orleans" and Bobby Darin's "Mack the Knife."

The nation was shocked to learn that a chartered plane crashed during an Iowa snowstorm, killing pop music stars Buddy Holly, Richie Valens, and The Big Bopper, as well as the plane's pilot.

On July 8, 1959, the Viet Cong attacked a U.S. Army unit near Bien Hoa, killing the first two Americans of the Vietnam War.

CHAPTER TWO

How Did War Define Us?

Flashing Back: Slogging Through the '60s

A presidential election held in **1960** pitted Republican Vice-President Richard M. Nixon against a young Democratic Senator from Massachusetts, John F. Kennedy. One of the most significant highlights was the first televised debate between presidential candidates in our nation's history. People who heard the debate on radio believed Nixon won. Those who watched it on television saw Kennedy as the winner. The Cold War was one of the major topics of the debate, with Kennedy making the so-called "missile gap" a primary campaign issue.

On May 1st of that year an American U-2 spy plane was shot down over the Soviet Union. At first, U.S. officials, including President Eisenhower, claimed the aircraft was a weather research plane leased to NASA.

However, members of the class soon learned that even the president could and would lie when the Soviets showed the plane's wreckage along with surveillance equipment and photos of Russian military bases. To top it off, they paraded before their television cameras the pilot, Francis Gary Powers, who was originally from Jenkins, Kentucky.

But the culture and the economy were still going strong at home. The top three popular television shows in 1960 were *The Andy Griffith Show, My Three Sons,* and *The Flintstones*. Three top songs of the year were "Theme From 'A Summer Place'" by Percy Faith,

"The Twist" by Chubby Checker, and "He'll Have To Go" by Jim Reeves.

←---→

John F. Kennedy became the 35th President of the United States in January **1961**. In his inaugural address, he urged Americans to "ask not what your country can do for you; ask what you can do for your country."

Barely into his presidency, Kennedy had to face three major challenges:
1) The Soviets sent the first person into space;
2) The CIA-backed Bay of Pigs invasion of Cuba failed;
3) The Berlin Wall was constructed.

In his book, McMaster noted that the new president decided on November 11, 1961, "to commit U.S. advisers to South Vietnam in excess of the number permitted in the Geneva Accords of 1954. Kennedy believed that increased Viet Cong activity in South Vietnam and Laos justified crossing that threshold."

That year, plentiful entertainment kept most Americans distracted from what was unfolding in southeast Asia. Some of the most popular television shows were *Wagon Train, Bonanza, Hazel,* and *Perry Mason.*

←---→

According to Karnow, in May **1962** U.S. Secretary of Defense Robert McNamara made his first trip to Vietnam. Known as a "numbers man," McNamara reportedly "looked at the figures and concluded optimistically after only forty-eight hours in the country that 'every quantitative measurement … shows that we are winning the war.'"

However, Hastings points to an opposite view of what might come: "An important 1962 Pentagon war game, SIGMA 1, estimated that half a million U.S. troops would be needed to defeat the Communists. A subsequent SIGMA 2 examined an air war option and concluded that no amount of bombing would deflect Hanoi. The conflicting evidence and projections put before policy-makers caused the various factions in Washington to box the compass with rival proposals, repeatedly changing their minds. Throughout the Kennedy era, Pentagon brass favored bombing the North but opposed the commitment of ground troops."

As Michael Maclear reports in his huge *Vietnam: A Complete Photographic History,* Kennedy, late in 1961 or early in 1962, had ordered the deployment of 300 American pilots to Vietnam. They "were ordered to lead the Vietnamese into battle but not to engage in combat—unless in self-defense." Maclear further noted that U.S. military advisors had increased to 4,000 by early 1962.

In October of that year, the world stood on the brink of nuclear war because of the Cuban Missile Crisis. The Soviets had installed missiles on the island country that is just 90 miles from the southernmost U.S. border. President Kennedy addressed the nation on television, showing photographic evidence of the missiles. U.S. military units were moved to Florida in the event of a possible invasion of Cuba, and a naval blockade was also put into place. Only after tense negotiations between the U.S. and the U.S.S.R. was war avoided.

Also that year, John Glenn became the first American to orbit the earth, actress Marilyn Monroe was found dead in her home in California, the oral polio vaccine was developed, and the first Walmart opened in Bentonville, Arkansas.

On television, popular shows were *American Bandstand, Dr. Kildare,* and *Candid Camera.* Walter Cronkite took over as anchor of the CBS Evening News.

Some of the most popular songs of 1962 were "Stranger On the Shore" by Mr. Acker Bilk, "I Can't Stop Loving You" by Ray Charles, and Dee Dee Sharp's "Mashed Potato Time."

Top movies were *Lawrence of Arabia, To Kill a Mockingbird* and *The Longest Day.*

Members of the Class of '66 entered high school in the fall of 1962. The Corbin High School Football Team finished the season as runners-up for the Kentucky State Championship. Also that year, the class and their fellow schoolmates got a first-hand look at racism. A sign at the town's city limits proclaimed that black people should "not let the sun set on their black skin." For decades the town had to live with that and other injustices imposed on African-Americans. During the school year 1962-1963, a young black man from nearby Pineville waited to change buses at Corbin. He asked the football coach, who was originally from Pineville, if he could shoot baskets in the gym while waiting. The coach agreed. That was in the morning. When students returned to school after lunch, they found that large numbers of their schoolmates had been pulled out by their parents. A community statement had been made.

←---→

The next year, **1963**, the class finished their freshman year and started their sophomore year. They listened to "Sugar Shack" by Jimmy Gilmer and The Fireballs, "Surfin' U.S.A." by The Beach Boys, and "Blowin' In The Wind" by Peter, Paul & Mary.

The online site *World History Projects* notes that early that year the small but very significant Battle of Ap Bac occurred. The battle resulted in what was seen as a major victory for the Viet Cong. The VC had 18 killed and 39 wounded, compared to the South Vietnamese who lost 80 to 100. Also, three American advisors lost their lives; eight were wounded. The VC used the victory for propaganda purposes, but "more importantly, they had successfully used tactics to counter the technological advantage the U.S. provided the South Vietnamese. This was done by being so close to the ARVN [Army of the Republic of Vietnam] and U.S. forces that they could not use air attacks without killing their own men." The website goes on to say that this success led the leadership in North Vietnam to "begin planning for a full-scale war in the South."

In the spring of 1963, several Buddhist uprisings against the government of Republic of Vietnam President Ngo Dinh Diem took place. That June, people around the world were horrified when they saw a picture of a Buddhist monk burning himself to death on the streets of Saigon to protest the government. Pressure increased on Kennedy to do something about the repressive tactics that Diem and his brother Ngo Dinh Nhu were inflicting on the populace of their own country.

After struggling with what to do, Kennedy told his ambassador in Saigon, Henry Cabot Lodge, that a change in government had to occur in South Vietnam. This information was relayed to a group of ARVN generals who had been plotting a coup, and early on November 2nd, Diem and his brother were killed.

Max Boot in his biography of CIA/U.S. Air Force Colonel Edward Lansdale, *The Road Not Taken*, said the coup and Diem's murder eliminated any chance of South Vietnam improving. "Dreams that South Vietnam would become a more liberal place were shattered as the new military dictators (those who took over after the coup) imposed strict censorship, shut down newspapers, and arrested anyone suspected of disloyalty. Martial law would be invoked far more often after Diem's demise than it had been while he was still in charge. Within weeks, thousands of students were marching in protests and more Buddhist monks than ever were immolating themselves in public. After years of nation building (which had been Lansdale's job when he worked with Diem in the mid-1950s), South Vietnam was returning to the chaos of the 1954-1955 period—just as Lansdale had warned would happen if Diem were removed."

Just three weeks after Diem's assassination, the intercom came on in Corbin High School. President Kennedy had been shot and killed in Dallas, Texas. School was dismissed.

Over the next several days members of the Class of '66 and their countrymen were glued to their televisions as they saw the somber aftermath of the assassination take place. It included the alleged killer, Lee Harvey Oswald, also being shot to death by businessman Jack Ruby in the basement of the Dallas Police Department.

That darkness was lifted somewhat in February **1964** when British pop group The Beatles appeared on *The Ed Sullivan Show*. Their appearance broke all existing television ratings records. The group went on to release five of the most popular songs of that year: at number 1, "I Want To Hold Your Hand"; at number 2, "She Loves You"; at number 13, "A Hard Day's Night"; at number 14, "Love Me Do"; and at number 16, "Please Please Me."

The three most popular television shows that year were *Bonanza, Bewitched,* and *Gomer Pyle, USMC*. The first Ford Mustang was produced.

Race relations were front and center. Riots erupted in New York, Chicago, Philadelphia, and other cities. Three civil rights workers disappeared in Mississippi after investigating the burning of an African-American church.

President Lyndon Johnson used his political skills to offer hope to black

Americans when The Civil Rights Act of 1964 was passed.

Johnson also was successful in gaining authorization from Congress to send American troops to Vietnam. The Gulf of Tonkin Resolution followed one (and possibly two) skirmishes between North Vietnamese torpedo boats and two American destroyers, USS Maddox and USS Turner Joy.

McMaster reports that Johnson went on national television after the incident. "He told Americans that 'aggression by terror against the peaceful villagers of South Vietnam has now been joined by open aggression on the high seas against the United States of America.'" He did not tell Americans that the U.S. had secretly been helping South Vietnamese saboteurs attack the North Vietnamese coast, which precipitated the release of the torpedo boats.

The U.S. Navy launched aircraft after the incident, attacking oil storage facilities and North Vietnamese naval vessels. One American pilot was shot down and killed; another, Lt. Everett Alvarez, Jr., ejected and was captured. He was the first American forced to survive captivity in North Vietnam.

Also in 1964, Kentuckian Cassius Clay (later Muhammed Ali) defeated Sonny Liston for the world heavyweight boxing championship. The Warren Commission released its report on the assassination of President Kennedy, concluding that Lee Harvey Oswald acted alone in the shooting. Nelson Mandela and seven other black South Africans were sentenced to life in prison. And Lyndon Johnson won a landslide victory over Sen. Barry Goldwater in the U.S. election for the presidency.

The members of the Class of '66 completed their sophomore year. After a summer of listening to The Beatles, they started their junior year. Vietnam was still a distant land with little or no meaning.

However, on November 1, 1964, Viet Cong guerrillas sneaked near the airfield at Bien Hoa and lobbed mortars for more than a half-hour. Four U.S.

servicemen were killed, with 72 wounded or injured. Of the thirty-six B-57 bombers stationed there, seventeen were damaged or destroyed.

←---→

February 7, **1965**, saw the VC launch a similar attack on an airfield and advisors' compound at Pleiku. According to McMaster, eight U.S. servicemen died and more than 100 were wounded. Twenty aircraft were set ablaze. In response, U.S. naval aircraft launched attacks on targets in the southern part of North Vietnam.

President Johnson, under pressure from "hawks" in his administration, decided that, with the attacks on Bien Hoa and Pleiku, the U.S. should send ground troops to South Vietnam to protect American assets. U.S. Marines landed near the coastal city of Danang in March. Johnson also approved a bombing campaign, later known as Rolling Thunder, against North Vietnam. According to Max Boot, Operation Rolling Thunder "… would dump more ordnance on North Vietnam than had been dropped on all of Europe in World War II."

Back home in Corbin, members of the Class of '66 were listening to "Wooly Bully" by Sam The Sham & The Pharaohs, "(I Can't Get No) Satisfaction" by the Rolling Stones, "Help!" by the Beatles, and "You've Lost That Lovin' Feelin'" by the Righteous Brothers.

Meanwhile, in his State of the Union address, Johnson unveiled his "Great Society" program, which included his "war on poverty." Malcolm X, influential black American Muslim minister and social activist, was assassinated in New York City. Alabama state troopers attacked civil rights demonstrators in Selma, Alabama—an incident that became known as "Bloody Sunday." As a result of that, Johnson crafted legislation and sent it to congress. When passed later in the year, it became known as the Voting Rights Act of 1965.

Motivated by racial tensions, the Watts Riots in Los Angeles lasted five days, leaving 34 dead and resulting in the arrests of 3,000 people.

The first SDS (Students for a Democratic Society) march against the

Vietnam War drew 25,000 protesters to Washington D.C.

Members of the Class of '66 saw troubling images on television that November, following the Battle of the Ia Drang Valley. This was the first major confrontation between regular troops of the United States and North Vietnam. Air assault troops had been dropped into an area where North Vietnamese soldiers were known to be. However, it quickly became obvious to the Americans that they were greatly outnumbered. U.S. troops prevailed after several days of bloody battle, only to leave the area. The North Vietnamese then returned. It was a pattern that would be followed throughout the war.

Hastings reports that on November 2nd an anti-war activist, 31-year-old Baltimore Quaker Norman Morrison, (in opposition to the war) "emulated the suicidal bonzes of Saigon, ritualistically burning himself to death outside [Defense Secretary Robert] McNamara's office window."

Boys in the Class of '66 started to pay attention to what was going on. They heard about punji sticks employed by the Viet Cong. These were sharpened sticks placed in holes that were concealed by brush. The VC smeared feces on the tips of the sticks so that if someone stepped on them, infection would set in.

The September 9, 1965, edition of *The Barbourville Mountain Advocate*, a southeastern Kentucky newspaper, reported that 90 young men from Knox County had been drafted. (Part of the city of Corbin is in Knox County.) The paper noted that the number of inductees was the largest for the region since the Korean War.

The boys in the Corbin High senior class knew that their futures were somehow going to be affected by that ever-widening war. In the spring, Jerry Elliott, Johnny Ratliff, Bob Underwood, and Ronnie Wyrick all signed up for delayed enlistment into the Air Force. After graduating in early June 1966, they left for basic training in Texas. Others signed up for the Army or awaited the draft. Many went to college, knowing that if that didn't work out, they too would soon be merely numbers in the military machine.

In fall 1965, President Johnson ordered an increase in troop strength in Vietnam from 75,000 to 125,000. He also ordered a doubling of the number of men to be drafted from 17,000 a month to 35,000.

←---→

It didn't take long for that number of troops in South Vietnam to increase again. By the end of January **1966**, there were 195,000 Americans serving there. In April, that jumped to 250,000. At the end of 1966, 385,300 Americans were serving in Vietnam, according to *Wikipedia*. That year also saw the largest number of men drafted (382,010) during the Vietnam War. The military draft was the major reason for opposition to the war.

Johnson sent Henry Cabot Lodge back to Vietnam as ambassador, replacing Maxwell Taylor. No fan of Lansdale, Lodge did agree to have him back in the country as the head of a liaison group between him and the South Vietnamese. One of his top priorities was to ensure a fair election for the Constituent Assembly in September. Boot says, "When Lodge heard about Lansdale's plans to stage a free election, he launched into a lengthy diatribe about how he and Lyndon Johnson had spent most of their lives rigging elections. 'Get it across to the press that they shouldn't apply higher standards here in Vietnam than they do in the U.S.,' he instructed aides. One of Lodge's closest aides believed that 'Lansdale wanted the reality of elections, while Lodge was convinced we needed only the appearance of a democracy in order to do what we had to do. Which wasn't the same thing.'"

Hastings reports that the U.S. had budgeted $2 billion for the war in 1966, but it ended up costing $15 billion. (That would rise to $17 billion in 1967.)

The cost on South Vietnam's civilian population was also on the rise. Hastings reports that on August 9, 1966, F-100s bombed a Delta community killing 63 civilians and wounding 51. Hastings quotes an American advisor as stating, "We killed an awful lot of people who didn't have anything to do with the war." He then cites news reporter Neil Sheehan asking Gen. William Westmoreland "if he was troubled by the civilian casualties caused by friendly fire. The general replied, 'Yes, Neil, it is a problem, but it does deprive the enemy of population, doesn't it?'"

Back home in the States, the Texas Western Miners defeated the Kentucky Wildcats for the men's national basketball championship. Texas Western had five black starters, while Kentucky's players were all white. The game is credited for beginning desegregation in athletic recruiting.

That fall, Bobby Seale and Huey P. Newton founded the Black Panther Party.

Top television shows in 1966 were *Star Trek, Mission Impossible, Batman,* and *The Monkees.* Popular songs were "The Ballad Of The Green Berets" by Sgt. Barry Sadler, "Cherish" by The Association, "Paperback Writer" by The Beatles, and The Rolling Stones' "Paint It Black."

And, of course, the Corbin Class of '66 graduated from high school, charging headlong into a very troubled world.

<---->

There were 485,600 Americans serving in Vietnam in **1967**. Operation Junction City was conducted between February 22 and May 14—the largest U.S. airborne operation since Operation Market Garden in World War II.

Two members of the Corbin Class of '66, Brian Engle and I, landed in Air Force basic training at Lackland AFB. Coming out of the chow hall one day in June, we saw a headline proclaiming that the Israelis and Arabs had gone to war. We thought, *Well it's either going to be Vietnam or the Middle East for us*. But that war only lasted six days, with Israel easily winning.

In 1967, The Beatles released their "Sgt. Pepper's Lonely Hearts Club Band" album.

Confrontations between black residents and the Detroit Police Department resulted in one of the worst "race riots" in U.S. history. The Detroit riots—July 23-31, 1967—left 43 people dead and 342 injured. More than 1,400 buildings were burned.

On July 30th, riots also broke out in Milwaukee, leading to a 10-day shutdown of that city.

On August 1st, riots spread to the nation's capital.

September 1967 in southeast Asia saw Nguyen Van Thieu elected president of South Vietnam.

Then, on October 26th, Navy pilot John McCain was shot down over North Vietnam. When he ejected, he broke both arms and a leg. He was immediately captured and spent more than five years in the infamous prison camp known as the Hanoi Hilton. He would survive and go on to be elected to the U.S. Senate many years later.

Some of the most popular songs in 1967 were "To Sir With Love" by Lulu, "Respect" by Aretha Franklin, "All You

Need Is Love" by The Beatles, and "The Letter" by The Box Tops. When Engle and I arrived at Sheppard AFB, we went to the Airmen's Club, drank 3.2 beer and sang along with our fellow buzzheads to "The Letter."

And then, there was **1968**.

Colonel Lansdale, according to historian Max Boot, believed the new year would be "pivotal." In a letter to Ambassador Ellsworth Bunker in October 1977, Lansdale said, "I believe that Hanoi is gambling on the climax of the war coming in 1968." Lansdale said he thought the North Vietnamese would try to repeat the success they'd had against the French following their victory at Dien Bien Phu, after which French public opinion forced an end to the war. "Dien Bien Phu was fought by the Viet Minh mostly to shape public opinion in Paris, a bit of drama rather than sound military strategy," Boot said. "It worked and made a handful of Vietnamese leaders famous inside the Communist world." Lansdale warned in his letter that "Hanoi was going to implement a similar plan to 'bleed the Americans' and 'get the American public to force U.S. withdrawal,' because 'they believe the American public is vulnerable to psychological manipulation in 1968.'"

President Johnson and his associates had been saying for years that we were winning in Vietnam. The war on television had shown the terrible costs, but most Americans believed that the president was telling them the truth.

All of that changed when, on the evening of January 31st, Communist forces violated the Tet (lunar new year) truce and launched coordinated attacks throughout all of South Vietnam. One of the most dramatic was the action against the U.S. embassy in Saigon. Television images showed Americans fighting Viet Cong guerrillas within the walls of the compound.

The next day, General William Westmoreland, commander of U.S. forces in Vietnam, tried to spin the events to explain away what was happening.

As Karnow reported, Westmoreland's "usual confidence" was largely ignored in American newspapers the following day when they printed a photograph of the Saigon police chief shooting a Viet Cong prisoner in the head. Americans could not ignore the horror of this war.

Just ten days before the Tet Offensive, North Vietnamese troops began an assault on Khe San, a U.S. Marine base in the highlands. Determined not to let it become America's Dien Bien Phu, President Johnson ordered that everything be thrown at the Communists. U.S. Air Force B-52 bombers saturated the area around the base, and "Puff the Magic Dragon" gunships raked enemy positions. Meanwhile, rockets, artillery shells, and mortars rained down on the Marines. The siege ended on April 8th when the North Vietnamese pulled out.

Also in Vietnam in 1968, the provincial capital of Hue was recaptured on February 24th after several weeks of street-to-street battle.

The My Lai Massacre occurred on March 16th, though it did not become known to the American public until 1969. American troops slaughtered scores of South Vietnamese civilians in the village of My Lai.

The Tet Offensive was officially declared *over* on September 23rd. The Viet Cong had been almost completely destroyed, but American public opinion had swung against the war, and support would not return.

There were 549,500 members of the U.S. military in Vietnam in 1968.

Hastings concludes that "hundreds of thousands of combat deaths from 1968 onward were especially tragic because they took place after the U.S. had abandoned hopes of victory and was battling merely to escape explicit defeat."

Members of the Class of '66—who were now in the military, college, or working—were listening to "Hey Jude" by The Beatles, "Mrs. Robinson" by Simon & Garfunkel, and "Sunshine of Your Love" by Cream.

Major events of the year included President Johnson announcing on March 31st that he would not seek re-election. Dr. Martin Luther King, Jr., was shot and killed in Memphis, Tennessee, on April 4th. Anti-war students took over administration buildings at Columbia University April 23-30. One million students marched through the streets of Paris on May 13th.

Presidential candidate and U.S. Senator Bobby Kennedy was shot in Los Angeles on June 5th; he died the next day.

During August 20–21, 1968, roughly 750,000 Warsaw Pact troops, 6,500 tanks and 800 aircraft invaded Czchoslovakia, thus ending the "Prague Spring," an attempt to break away from Communist domination.

The Democratic National Convention was held August 22-30 in Chicago, resulting in police clashing with anti-war protesters in the streets and mayhem breaking out in the convention hall.

Former Vice-President Richard Nixon defeated Vice-President Hubert Humphrey in the presidential election that fall.

Then, the whole world witnessed a modern miracle: Apollo 8 entered orbit around the moon on December 24, 1968.

←---→

In **1969**, some of the popular music included the Fifth Dimension's "Aquarius/Let The Sunshine In," "I Can't Get Next To You" by the Temptations, and the Beatles' "Let It Be."

Members of the Class of '66 turned 21.

The war in Southeast Asia raged on.

CHAPTER THREE

What Can Stories Teach Us?

Flashing Forward: Class of '66 in Our Own Words

Rick Scalf was a close friend of both Brian Engle and me. Like us, he had gone to Eastern Kentucky University in the fall of 1966. Unlike us, Rick would remain in school and graduate.

"I was aware of it (the war) in high school, but it didn't affect me until my cousin joined the Army and went to Vietnam," Scalf said.

Rick Scalf

"He came back okay, but he bragged about spending a week in the hospital due to catching VD from Vietnamese prostitutes.

"I recall all of the TV and other media accounts of the many U.S. soldiers' deaths, and the destruction there, including Saigon.

"I became more aware after you [this author] and Wayne [Brian Wayne Engle] left college. A lot of campus discussions were held, and some unrest occurred. There was no violence that I know of. Peter Jennings of ABC [News] came to EKU and interviewed then President Robert Martin regarding his ability to keep the campus peaceful and under control. The interview was on national news one night."

Mona Dean

Mona Dean went to Berea College in the fall of 1966, along with her best friend **Donna Cash**, to study nursing.

She said she really didn't think about Vietnam until she was in college. "I always thought about Matt and the other boys. I didn't think of them in a political context."

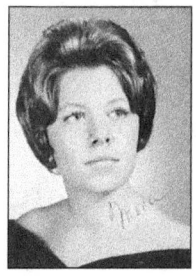
Mona Dean '66

She was touched directly by the war because her older brother served two tours in Vietnam. When he came back, she said, "He went into rages. That was my first real experience with PTSD."

Jayne Moore Goodin Sears says she was aware of the war while in high school and was opposed to it: "It was about boys, not men."

Her first husband, Dennis Goodin, had been in the Class of '65. He attended nearby Cumberland College, but decided he wanted to join the Marines. He signed up, but a family friend, the local Army recruiter, intervened and had him transferred to the Army. In December 1966, Goodin left and, after training as a medic, was sent to Thailand. According to Jayne,

Dennis would periodically be sent on temporary duty to Vietnam.

"He wouldn't talk about it," Jayne said about Goodin's experiences, "but he started taking drugs and drinking. Once, he tried to shoot out the street lights."

"In March or April [1966] I made up my mind that I would join," **Jerry Elliott** said in an interview.

Jerry Elliott '66

"I didn't want to go to college at that time, and I had a high draft number.

"One week after graduation, we were in San Antonio [Lackland Air Force Base]."

After basic, Elliott was sent to Sheppard AFB near Wichita Falls, Texas, for aircraft maintenance training. **Ronnie Wyrick** was sent straight out of basic to his first permanent duty station in Nevada, as was **Bob Underwood**, who went to North Dakota. Wyrick was later sent to South Korea, and Underwood went to Turkey.

Elliott's first permanent duty station was at a base near Clovis, New Mexico. One day he got orders for Vietnam. He was sent to Tuy Hoa to work on F100 Super Sabre jets, and stayed there for 365 days—from October 12, 1968, to October 12, 1969.

Elliott was discharged early, and said he came home to Corbin the same day that **Matt Stewart**'s remains arrived. Looking back, Elliott said of his time in Vietnam, "I thought we were pussy-footing around," referring to the U.S. "strategy." After all of these years, he said, "We shouldn't have been there."

Matt Stewart '66

Johnny Ratliff went into the Air Force at the same time as Jerry Elliot. His basic training was elsewhere in Texas, and his first permanent duty station was at Davis–Monthan AFB, near Tucson, Arizona. Ratliff was a maintenance control airman, preparing flight schedules and keeping maintenance records on F4C fighter jets. His entire tour was spent at Davis–Monthan.

Arlo Sharp was valedictorian of the Class of '66. Intelligent, sensitive, and thoughtful, Sharp responded to my request for an interview by writing an essay.

Arlo Sharp

"I first heard of Vietnam," Sharp wrote, "in Mrs. Neva Pennington's fifth grade class at Central Elementary school in Corbin, Kentucky, in the academic year 1958-1959.

"Our geography textbook contained a unit on southeast Asia. We learned about the Malay peninsula and tropical rainforest through the eyes of a fictitious native boy named Bunga. And we boys who lived in my neighborhood of vacant lots and woodsy areas played at being Bunga, with our loincloths and reed spears.

"Fast forward to my high school

junior year, spring 1965. A lady from our local draft board spoke in assembly at Corbin High. She talked about the war in Vietnam, but it seemed remote, nothing that affected us. However, as my senior year arrived, more and more news on television concerned Vietnam.

"In April 1966, I turned eighteen and registered for the military draft. When asked about identifying marks or scars, I indicated a scar on my right wrist, result of a close encounter with a broken Pepsi bottle several years before. The secretary recorded it on my registration card. Later I realized such information might be used to help identify my body. I still have the card. And the scar.

"Graduation came, and some of my classmates entered the armed forces. In the fall of 1966, I enrolled in college. College students received draft deferments, but that wasn't why I went. From a young age, I'd been oriented to attend college. But evidently a lot of young men attended to avoid the draft. I'm not saying they shouldn't have, but many were not prepared for college study. Under different circumstances, they'd have entered the work force instead. And male students knew if they failed and dropped out of college, they would likely be drafted and sent to Vietnam. I saw it happen more than once.

Arlo Sharp '66

"After their service, some returned to school. And some did not return at all.

"As the 1960s progressed, some local young men became casualties of the Vietnam War. One was Marine Lieutenant Gary Holtzclaw. On the day of his funeral, I drove by the church and saw the flag display.

"Also David Durham, a neighborhood boy younger than me. We'd played together as children.

"Later, the first classmate, **Matt Stewart**. I saw him for the last time in spring 1968, during a pick-up basketball game at Felts Elementary School playground.

"And another classmate, **Jackie Trosper**. He once gave me a ride in this boxy little sports car. It may have been a Chevy Corvair.

"During my college years, I followed the news out of Vietnam. I remember the daily casualty reports, the number of Americans killed versus the number of North Vietnamese and Viet Cong. The numbers sounded so lopsided in our favor that I wondered why the enemy didn't run out of soldiers. Later I would hear that the casualty lists were often inflated and sometimes included dead animals."

Sharp is referring to the weekly numbers released by the U.S. Department of Defense noting American and South Vietnamese dead, as well as North Vietnamese and Viet Cong soldiers killed.

Defense Secretary Robert McNamara and General William Westmorland, the American commander in Vietnam, saw success through statistics. Therefore, the more enemy deaths, compared to American and South Vietnamese losses, was seen in win/loss ratio terms. A large enemy body count meant success.

U.S. officers knew that their future promotions depended on high body counts, even if the numbers were inflated. *Wikipedia* cites historian Christian Appy who wrote: "One study revealed that 61 percent of American commanders considered that body counts were grossly exaggerated." The Department of Defense says 950,765 Communist forces were killed in Vietnam from 1965 to 1974. However, an estimated 220,000 of those were civilians killed by either U.S. or South Vietnamese forces.

Sharp's essay continues:

"As my college years continued and graduation neared, a mood of despair gripped me. Although I was a good student and never in danger of failing, I found myself afraid I might flunk out and wind up in Vietnam. Never a sound sleeper, I had even more trouble resting well at night. And I asked myself why I bothered doing difficult college work when after graduation I'd be sent halfway across the world to die. When someone asked me what I planned to do after graduation, I answered that I expected to be drafted.

"World War Two lasted less than four years; why was this war dragging on and on? No one seemed to know exactly when or how it started, what its objective was, and when we'd achieve victory, if ever.

"An uncle who served in the south Pacific during World War II remarked that we were fighting an undeclared war and were not doing so effectively. If we were going to fight a war, we should obtain a congressional declaration of war and go in with all our might and win it. I couldn't help but wonder why that hadn't already been accomplished.

"As significant numbers of the American people turned against the Vietnam War, I suppose I did so, too. But I never disrespected any soldier who served. They followed orders given by our government. Whether our government should've given those orders is another question, and I cannot answer it.

"A cartoon of the era showed a sergeant and a raw recruit standing in a field of identical shoulder-high mushrooms. Pointing left and right, the sergeant says, 'Now these are the mushrooms and those are the toadstools. The mushrooms are friends, and the toadstools are the enemy.'

"'But how can I tell the difference?' asks the recruit.

"'You'll know it's a toadstool when it kills you!' says the sergeant.

"And that seemed to be the way of it. A war against a ruthless, faceless enemy, among natives who often hated us and were enemies themselves, and rules of engagement which favored the enemy. Stories came out about young girls with grenades strapped under their clothes being sent to ask American GIs for candy. And of young children being killed by the Viet Cong because they accepted candy or other gifts from our soldiers.

"The attitude of some college students irritated me, although I did not confront them. Not my nature. An attractive girl, daughter of a career Air Force officer, asserted that if she were a boy, she'd be over there fighting. *Easy to say*, I thought, *when you're not carrying a draft card and you'll never have to go unless you choose to*. We males of that era did not want women to serve in combat, but I've often wondered if after graduation she chose to go, perhaps become a nurse. Somehow, I doubt it.

"In 1969, the draft lottery occurred. Our family watched television the night the numbers were drawn. I was thankful my younger brother drew a number in the three-hundred-forty range. He'd never have to worry about going to war. But I drew number eighty-one. Still, if someone had to serve, I'd rather it be me. One feels protective of younger siblings. During those years, my mom worried herself sick that one of us would have to go. A young teenager in World War II, she had four brothers serving at the same time. All came back, but one was wounded. I have his purple heart.

"In 1968, I had voted in a presidential election for the first time. Among other promises, Richard Nixon indicated he'd end the war in Vietnam. Of course, he did not. Some said too much money was being made by industrial military suppliers—war is good economic times as long as your side is winning and someone else is on the front line facing the bullets. I recall some televised congressional hearings about overcharges, shoddy materials, or something of that nature. If I remember correctly, a uniformed officer took the Fifth Amendment more than thirty times during the questioning.

"On one occasion a war correspondent spoke in assembly at my college. Having been to Vietnam, he revealed something that stuck in my mind. At that time, the United States and North Vietnam were engaging in peace talks. According to the speaker, the Vietnamese considered the peace negotiations as part of the war, something in which to gain an advantage. I seem to recall that the Vietnamese envoys argued over the size and shape of the negotiating table.

"In spring 1970, I did student teaching at London [Kentucky] High School. One day the news came that the fiancé of a student had been killed in Vietnam. An excellent student, the girl still attended school the next day. But about mid-morning, she broke down. A lady teacher embraced her as she sobbed in the hallway. As I watched, I thought: *Damn Richard Nixon, damn Lyndon Johnson, damn anyone who'd cause this young girl such pain and heartbreak.* That one American life was worth more than all the people in Southeast Asia combined.

"A short time later, my supervising teacher informed me that another former student had been lost in Vietnam. The teacher, also a minister, told me he'd talked to the boy's parents. The father said his son had a job and a girlfriend, and they were talking marriage. And our government took him over there and killed him. For nothing.

"The Kent State University shootings occurred while I was student teaching. The cavalier attitude expressed by some teachers shocked me. Few of them seemed to care that Americans had killed other Americans. In the faculty lounge, one lady said she felt no sympathy whatever as she saw television images of the bodies lying on the grass. Of course, she wasn't facing the draft and would never have any reason to protest the war, but I did not argue with her. In any case, I could never look upon young lives cut short and the subsequent years of heartache for their loved ones without emotion. Later I'd learn two of those killed at Kent State took no part in the antiwar demonstration, and one was a member of the campus ROTC battalion."

Sharp is referring here to the May 4, 1970, shootings at Kent State University in Ohio. On the evening of April 30th, President Nixon had announced on national television an invasion of Cambodia. U.S. and South Vietnamese forces attempted to defeat the approximately 40,000 North Vietnamese and Viet Cong troops using that country as a sanctuary and staging area. Following the announcement of the invasion, campuses across the U.S. erupted in demonstrations, as the action was seen as a widening of the war. The governor of Ohio ordered National Guard troops to Kent State to quell demonstrations on that campus. According to *Wikipedia*, 28 guardsmen fired approximately 67 rounds of live ammunition into the crowd of unarmed students over a period of 13 seconds. Four students were killed and nine were injured. Four million college students across the country went on strike following the event.

Just two months before the Kent State shootings, **Brian Engle** was at Phan Rang, an Air Force fighter base north of Saigon. That March 4th was a sunny day, and Engle was in the middle of the base around four in the afternoon, not yet on duty as a computer technician, when the rockets started falling. He said he "heard a pop" and

Brian Engle

"found I was sitting." He had been hit in the left arm and both thighs with shrapnel. A friend put a belt around the more serious arm wound to serve as a tourniquet.

Some of those around him were killed. Engle spent close to a month at the Air Force hospital at Cam Ranh, healing. Of the experience, he said, "It helped me make up my mind that if I'm going to get killed I should do something that has more meaning. I almost got killed doing something I considered of no value [the computer work]."

Because of his 13-month tour in country, Engle said, he had a ticket to retrain for another job. He re-enlisted and trained as a tail gunner of B-52 bombers. He would serve three more tours in that capacity, flying out of Guam and Thailand over both South and North Vietnam.

Arlo Sharp picks up with his memories:

"I recall the television coverage of the My Lai Massacre, and the subsequent conviction of Lieutenant William Calley. My father always watched the news, and he had strong opinions that Calley should've been 'hanged from the highest tree,' as he put it. When Calley wasn't sentenced to death and later was pardoned, it angered my dad.

"Sometime afterwards, news would come out about American officers who engaged in a sport called 'gook-hunting,' which made me wonder if My Lai was akin to that."

As noted earlier, the My Lai massacre occurred in 1968, but did not become publicly known until 1969.

Max Hastings, writing about the massacre, says that public dismay eventually "swelled to a flood tide. Nonetheless, 23rd Division staff officer Maj. Colin Powell, later U.S. Secretary of State, produced a memorandum for the adjutant general that was an uncompromising whitewash, asserting that 'relations between American soldiers and the Vietnamese people are excellent.'"

A member of the U.S. Army Third Infantry Division, Tom Sampson, posted the following information on December 8, 2016:

"Operation Iron Mountain was a unilateral and combined operation with ARVN and provincial forces in the Quang Ngai Province to find, fix and destroy enemy main force and local force units in the 11th Brigade's TAOR (Tactical Area of Responsibility) and TAOI (Tactical Area of Interest) and to interdict enemy supply and communication lines.

"On September 21, 1969, Alpha Company 4-3 Infantry used a night defense position which they had previously occupied during the operation. Unbeknownst to them, the enemy had bracketed the position, and at 1905 hours (7:05 p.m.) their location received thirty 82 mm mortar rounds and small arms fire from all around the perimeter. Three of the mortar rounds landed directly in foxholes.

"Alpha Company initially reported four U.S. KHA (killed hostile action) and five WHA (wounded hostile action).

At 2000 hours (8 p.m.) that report was amended when Alpha Company added seven more KHA and six more WHA for a total of 11 U.S. KHA and 11 U.S. WHA. All of the KHA had been occupying the foxholes bracketed by the mortar fire.

"The first dustoff (medical evacuation by helicopter) for six U.S. WHA was completed at 2000 hours. At 2100 hours (9 p.m.), Alpha Company reported the 11 KHA, and 10 WHA were dusted off with one WHA remaining in the field due to minor wounds."

Among the 11 KHA was Spec. 4 **Henry M. Stewart, Jr.**, from Corbin, Kentucky.

Sampson knew the details of what happened because as a member of the First Platoon of Company A, he was there.

Just three weeks before Stewart was killed, North Vietnam's leader Ho Chi Minh died on September 2, 1969.

Sharp's essay continues:

"In a major magazine of the era, I saw some photographs of wounded soldiers. The most stomach-churning picture showed something I didn't recognize at first. I finally realized it was the side view of a young man's face. Except he had no face. No eyes, no nose, no mouth. A bloody crater of mangled flesh extended from his hairline to his chin.

"In March 1970, I and others my age, including several classmates, received a notice to report for our military pre-induction physicals. A bus would take us from the Greyhound station in Williamsburg, Kentucky, to the armed forces induction center in Knoxville, Tennessee, for exams. I drove from Corbin to Williamsburg, and three other guys rode with me: **Micaiah Bailey**, **Wayne Frazier**, and **Gerald Cassidy**. On the way, the four of us were talking, laughing and cracking jokes. Gerald remarked that on the way back we would not be feeling so cheerful. Of course, he was right.

"At the bus station, draft board secretary Mrs. Jeanette Hudson called the roll. When she spoke the name of a certain classmate, no one answered. She called it again. Still nothing. She looked puzzled, then jotted down a note. In that era, not showing up for an official military notice was practically an unpardonable sin. I wondered how the guy got away with it. He was related to prominent people in the Corbin area, and perhaps that explains it."

A side note here:

When asked about her experience with the Vietnam War, one classmate told me that her husband-to-be avoided military service because his prominent grandmother, who had connections with Republican politicians, made some calls. When asked for more details, the classmate did not return emails or calls.

Arlo Sharp continues:

"Afterwards, Mrs. Hudson spoke a few words of encouragement, and a couple of ministers said a prayer for us. One guy whispered that not even God could help us at that point.

"At the induction center, we were herded around like cattle. For the urine test, I had difficulty producing any because we stood two at a time at a urinal, and I find it difficult to urinate in anyone else's presence. Several guys came and went beside me before I finally prevailed. On the hearing test, also a two-person station, I found myself distracted by the guy beside me continually clicking his handheld device, which one did upon hearing certain sounds through the earphones.

"After the exams, everyone gathered in a large assembly hall. A sergeant seated at a desk in front called the names of those who didn't pass the physical. They walked forward one at a time.

"A huge guy waddled to the front and back. As he regained his seat, someone asked, 'What kind of taters you been eating?'

"'Big'uns, buddy,' he answered. 'Big'uns!'

"One classmate, who'd brought a sheaf of papers about his medical conditions 'like the Sears & Roebuck catalog,' as another classmate put it, turned to face the assembly and grinned. Spreading his hands wide apart in the well-known baseball signal, he said, 'Safe!'

"'We oughta make that son-of-a-bitch walk back to Corbin,' whispered the other classmate.

"One guy was asthmatic. As he told us later, an officer asked him how an attack felt. His mind went blank for a moment before he replied, 'Sir, it's like being smothered with a pillow.'

"'Okay, son,' said the officer. 'We'll take you right after we take the women and children.'"

By the end of 1970, the United States had 335,790 troops still in Vietnam. That was down from the 549,500 in 1968 and 1969. However, the draft was still lively, though it was the lottery version.

Sharp addressed that in a continuation of his essay:

"My draft lottery number cost me a graduate assistantship at the University of Kentucky, which I'd been awarded during my college senior year. With my low number, I'd be drafted immediately after graduation. But I focused on going to graduate school, as I wanted to become a college professor. After a talk with my college counselor Dr. Fred Roth and local minister Dr. Raymond Lawrence, I decided to attend Southern Baptist Theological Seminary in Louisville. Divinity students were deferred from military service, whereas regular graduate students were not. After being accepted, I gave up my assistantship to UK. In fall of 1970, I enrolled at Southern.

"I've often asked myself if I went to a theological school just to avoid the draft. Without a doubt, that was part of the consideration. But I'd grown up in a religious home and tried to be cognizant of the Almighty. I always had a strong conscience and sense of guilt. And it's easy to convince oneself of God's will when other benefits accrue. In any event, seminary didn't work out for me. I dropped out in early November."

Eric Burdon and The Animals had released the anti-war song "Sky Pilot" in 1968. It's about military chaplains who sent troops off to battle with a prayer. Members of the U.S. military applied the term "Sky Pilot" derisively to the large number of men of their generation who found religion and became ministers so they could avoid service.

Sharp continues:

"I came home and appealed my draft status to the state board, a delaying action more than anything else. One evening a local draft board member phoned me. He told me my appeal was worthless without a specific reason. I explained about the old knee injury and told him I needed time to see an orthopedic specialist. I'd had an appointment in October but had to reschedule to December because of a bout of flu. The man instructed me to call the secretary of the draft board and explain to her. I told him I would, but I did not. And again, I'm not sure why —perhaps due to my fatalistic outlook. I sat on the couch and wept. At the time, it seemed like nothing much mattered. I felt powerless, with no control over my destiny; as if vast, impersonal forces held my existence in their hands and could snuff it out in a heartbeat, or on a whim. A life full of promise on college graduation day the previous spring appeared to have gone down the drain."

Sharp eventually saw the orthopedist who agreed to write a letter describing the knee issue as a "soft tissue problem" but the letter "did not contain a specific recommendation for deferral of military service." Sharp mailed it to the draft board.

"But shortly afterwards my draft notice arrived in the mail. My mom opened the envelope. I was ordered to report to the Williamsburg Greyhound bus station at 7 a.m. on Tuesday, February 2, 1971. The envelope also contained a new draft card classifying me as 1-A, with the notation that the state appeals board had met and voted against my appeal six to zero. And a note said my letter from the doctor had been forwarded to the armed forces induction center in Knoxville.

"During that time, I also paid a visit to our family doctor, a World War II veteran. I told him about the emotional turmoil I was experiencing, how I didn't think I could cope with military service. I broke down and cried in front of him. It seemed to embarrass him. He gave me a pep talk, told me the military wouldn't *ask* me to adjust; they'd *tell* me to adjust. I wanted to tell him I felt my life was essentially over, that there was no longer any point to anything. I'd been having suicidal thoughts, but could not bring myself to mention it. And my thoughts were probably not serious, although they'd return later.

"For some time after that, every time the doctor saw me, he'd ask if I'd gotten over my 'nervous trouble.' I always answered yes. And eventually I did.

"I tried to prepare myself to become a member of the armed forces—with the certain knowledge that I would not be coming back, which I'm sure every prospective young soldier believes. It was common in that era for young couples to marry quickly and, after a short honeymoon, the husband was off to Vietnam. But I did not feel I could subject a girl to that kind of uncertainty, and during that time I never tried to cultivate a serious relationship.

"On February 1st, I talked to my grandfather, my mother's dad. I told him I had to go the army the next day and might not see him for a while. He showed concern. Maybe he remembered his four sons in World War II.

"'Hope you get along good, best in the world,' he said.

"In the evening I packed my bag with a razor, underwear, socks, etc. That night I stayed up late to finish a library book, *Night Without End* by Scottish author Alistair MacLean, who had also written such novels as *The Guns of Navarone* and *Where Eagles Dare*. Several books would be due back at the Corbin Public Library later in the week. My brother said he would return them for me. Many years later, I would buy that same copy of *Night Without End* during a Corbin Library book sale, and I still have it. Seems appropriate, somehow.

"I did not rest much during the night. In the morning my mom fixed an early breakfast for my dad and me. He'd be driving me to Williamsburg. My dad went outside to start the car. The day was bitterly cold. Resigned but dry-eyed, I said goodbye to my mom at the back door.

"'See you later, I reckon,' I told her.

"She hugged me and quickly ran into the other part of the house, I thought to cry or maybe to pray. Or both. My dad drove me to Williamsburg and let me out beside the bus station.

"He patted me on the shoulder and said, 'Take care now. Be careful.'

"'Okay,' I said as I felt tears coming on. 'Okay.'

"Not wanting to cry in front of him, I quickly entered the station—just then realizing that day was my dad's fifty-first birthday.

"I had folded and put a copy of the doctor's letter in my jacket pocket. Maybe they had received the copy at the induction center, but maybe not.

"A few other guys waited inside. I recognized brothers Curt and Danny Smith, who'd grown up in Corbin and attended school there. They were drinking coffee. A veteran, Curt was a few years older than me, and he'd married **Nancy Dooley**, a classmate. Danny was three years younger. Seeing people I knew helped my peace of mind.

"'Hey Curt,' I said. 'Are you going back in?'

"'No,' he replied with a smile. 'Danny here is.'

"Danny grinned and lifted his cup in greeting. I wondered if he was as worried as I was. I visited the restroom. Maybe nerves, but I had morbid thoughts as I emptied my bladder.

"*The bridge over the Cumberland River is only a hundred yards or so away. You could slip out the back, walk over there, stroll midway across, and step over the side. As cold as that water is, you wouldn't last any time at all…*

"I returned to the waiting room. Mrs. Hudson arrived and spoke to us, and a minister prayed for us. I was a person of faith then (and still am), but God seemed far away. The bus arrived. It had come from Pineville, bringing some guys from that area.

"On the way to Knoxville, I sat beside a younger guy. I was twenty-two at the time, and he looked seventeen or eighteen. I asked if he was going for a pre-induction physical, but he answered that he was going into service. I could tell he was afraid. I don't remember his name, if I knew it, but I hope he did okay.

"During the trip, I needed to visit the vehicle's bathroom. Nerves again. I walked past a couple of rough-looking guys in the back. They glared at me. I nodded and smiled, said a few innocuous words. They glared harder. Bully-types, maybe.

"And I'd been bullied in grade school, high school and college. Looked like military service wouldn't be much different. Fatalism again.

"I sat down on the tiny toilet and urinated. When I finished and stood, I saw to my horror that the doctor's letter had slipped out of my jacket pocket and fallen into the receptacle. But it was wedged in a rubber strip above the water line and hadn't gotten wet. I quickly retrieved it.

"We arrived in Knoxville and took seats in the big assembly room. From there I was shown to a dressing room and instructed to strip down to my underwear, then report to a sergeant in the next room.

"When I stood in my undies before his desk, he asked without glancing up, 'Any change in your health?'

"'Yes,' I replied, 'I have this letter.'

"I asked him if they'd received a copy of it from my local draft board. He said they had not. For some reason, that didn't surprise me. And I had no expectations the letter would be considered for a moment. The sergeant read it and underlined several words. Handed it back and instructed me to take it to an officer in the next room.

I did so. The officer read it and also did some underlining. He looked up at me.

"'You don't go because of that knee, bud,' he said.

"'Oh,' I said. 'Okay.'

"Astonished, I thought something inane: *You mean I don't get to go?*"

Sharp then tells about the rest of the day, eating at the cafeteria, meeting up with other guys who failed their physicals, including Danny Smith, and going back to Williamsburg and on to Corbin.

Sharp says, "In a few days I received a new draft card classifying me to 1-Y, subject to military service only during a national emergency. The next year I was reclassified to 4F, unfit for any military service."

The 1971 that Sharp wrote about included such war developments as the South Vietnamese invasion of Laos backed by U.S. air and artillery support, the publication of the Pentagon Papers, and 500,000 people turning out for an anti-war demonstration in Washington, D.C.

Elsewhere that year, Charles Manson and three of his followers were found guilty in the 1969 Tate–LaBianca murders, Intel released the world's first microprocessor, and the 26th Amendment to the U.S. Constitution was signed, changing the voting age from 21 to 18. Those who had heretofore been drafted into the military had previously had no say in who should order them to war.

Popular music of the year included "Joy to the World" by Three Dog Night, "Maggie May"/"Reason to Believe" by Rod Stewart, and Carole King's "It's Too Late"/"I Feel the Earth Move."

The following year, 1972, pop radio was playing Roberta Flack's "The First Time Ever I Saw Your Face," Don McLean's "American Pie," and "Alone Again (Naturally)" by Gilbert O'Sullivan.

In war news, the last draft lottery was held on February 2nd. According to *Wikipedia*, none of those men were ever called for service. On March 30th, North Vietnamese troops crossed the DMZ into South Vietnam. Because of that, the U.S.

resumed bombing Hanoi and Haiphong. President Nixon announced on June 28th that no more draftees would be sent to Vietnam.

Film actress Jane Fonda visited North Vietnam in July and was photographed sitting on an anti-aircraft gun. She has forever since been derisively called "Hanoi Jane."

The U.S. lost its first B-52 bomber in the war on November 22, 1972—the ninth anniversary of the assassination of President John F. Kennedy.

Also that year, five White House political operatives had been arrested (June 17th) for burglarizing the Democratic National Committee's headquarters in the Watergate building in Washington, D.C. That fall, Richard Nixon won re-election to a second term as U.S. President in a landslide victory over Sen. George McGovern, who was an anti-war candidate.

Brian Engle's first four years of duty had ended in 1971, and (as previously mentioned) he had re-enlisted in order to retrain as a tail-gunner on a B-52. That

Brian Wayne Engle '66

would lead to three more tours in the combat area with his aircraft flying out of either Guam or Thailand.

Most B-52 duty was in South Vietnam in an action called Arc Light. The program was in support of ground action and included the bombing of enemy ground forces and their transportation of supplies. Attacks in North Vietnam were mostly in the southern part of the country, though those in the Hanoi and Haiphong areas were proving to be effective.

Marshall L. Michel III, in his book *The 11 Days of Christmas,* says, "Suffering from military setbacks and with their allies wavering (Nixon had made inroads with both China and the Soviet Union), the North Vietnamese in mid-October made more concessions to Kissinger in Paris. By October 21, 1972, both sides had agreed to a draft peace agreement to be signed ten days later. Kissinger felt the agreement met

U.S. aims—the South Vietnamese government was left intact, all the fighting in Indochina would end, there would be no more infiltration of South Vietnam, North Vietnamese troops would leave Laos and Cambodia, and all U.S. prisoners of war would be returned and Americans missing in action would be accounted for."

Because of that, Kissinger advised Nixon to halt the bombing. The president reluctantly agreed, but only for the northern third of North Vietnam.

The Americans were then faced with the difficult task of trying to convince the South Vietnamese leadership of the proposed agreement—an agreement that would have left North Vietnamese troops in the South.

Michel says, "Kissinger lamented: 'We face the paradoxical situation that the North, which has effectively lost, is acting as if they had won, while the South, which has effectively won, is acting as if it has lost.'"

South Vietnamese President Thieu rejected the plan, saying that all Northern troops must leave the South.

With an October 31, 1972, deadline looming for the agreement to be approved, Nixon decided he did not want to appear as if he were abandoning his ally when his own reelection was only a few weeks away. He decided to put more pressure on the North by increasing shipments of weapons to the South and ordering B-52 strikes in a northerly direction.

Michel picks up the story:

"The North Vietnamese—with some justification—felt betrayed. Not only had the United States not signed the agreement on the agreed date, but it was also increasing its bombing, sending more equipment to South Vietnam, and demanding the negotiations be reopened to revise the agreement Kissinger negotiated in October. Adding to the North Vietnamese chagrin was the fact that Viet Cong units had come out of hiding in many places in South Vietnam at the end of October to try to lay claims to territory in anticipation of the October 31 cease-fire signing. When there was no cease-fire, the South Vietnamese forces decimated them."

Nixon easily won reelection, but Democrats made major gains in the Congress. There were going to be more anti-war members of the Senate in January, and the president and Kissinger knew that something would have to be done before then. Kissinger told Nixon that if agreement could not be reached between the U.S. and the two Vietnams, "...we will have to resume massive bombing and take the position that our only objective henceforth will be U.S. military disengagement in return for the release of our prisoners ... we have proven it is impossible to negotiate a more comprehensive settlement because of the implacability of the two Vietnamese sides."

The Strategic Air Command (SAC) was very set in its ways as to how B-52s should be operated. Since 1967, SAC had required that planes use the same tactics of airspeeds, altitudes, jamming patterns and formations on all operations. The North Vietnamese learned this and knew that the big bombers flew in long streams along the same routes. Their Surface-to-Air Missile (SAM) crews believed they could knock down the B-52s and, as noted earlier, they did so on November 22, 1972. However, according to Michel, they were frustrated because the planes did not crash in Vietnam, but made it to Thailand before going down.

Frustrated with both the North and South Vietnamese governments, Nixon ordered military leaders to plan for B-52 raids on Hanoi. Michel says Nixon told them, "The strike plan ... must be so configured as to create the most massive shock effect in a psychological context." He ordered the bombing to begin on the 17th of December, but it was later moved to the 18th.

Late in the afternoon of December 18, 1972, the crews of the BUFFs arrived for briefings. Brian Engle remembered it as life imitating art, recalling the movie *12 O'Clock High*, and the scene where the B-17 crews, seeing a curtain pulled back, are told their target is Berlin. "A curtain was pulled back and we were told, 'Gentlemen, the target tonight is Hanoi,'" Engle said in an interview. "I remember looking around and thinking, 'Some of us aren't going to be here tomorrow.'"

Engle had not been back in Guam very long. He had been home on leave when his father died on November 15. He had planned to get an impacted tooth fixed while he was home, but the untimely death had changed his plans.

Because of the dental problem, Engle was listed as not being cleared to fly. However, he was not about to let his crew fly on the momentous trip into Hanoi without him. "I said, 'g..d….. I'm going.'"

He went to the flight surgeon's office and found it closed. After banging on the door, someone appeared, and Engle was told the doctor was not going to put anyone on the list of unavailable airmen.

"I don't want *on* the list," he said, "I want *off*." Five minutes later, he was cleared and went to the briefing.

Engle's plane was the second in a small group of three known as a cell. His cell had a call sign of Charcoal, and his aircraft was Charcoal 2. According to Michel, the Charcoal cell and two others following were tasked with the bombing of the Yen Vien railroad. As they were arriving on target and Charcoal 1 opened its bomb bay doors, a SAM hit the plane. This was followed shortly by another hit. The pilot was instantly killed, and the plane went down.

"Flying back to Guam that night I was struck with how beautiful the world was, how beautiful the Pacific was," said Engle, aware of how close he had come to death.

"When I got back, I was thinking that Mom would be hearing about our mission and our losses from Walter Cronkite. I knew she would be worried. After debriefing, I called her long-distance, and she picked right up. I told her that Guam was boring, and she believed it. As far as she knew, I was on the beach reading a book."

Engle next participated in the December 22nd bombing, which he said was not as memorable as the flight on the 18th had been. He called that trip on the 22nd "stupid" because SAC ordered the same tactics used on the same targets.

His final trip during Linebacker Two was on December 26th. He says it was "much better" because SAC listened to Brig. Gen. Glenn Sullivan, who had said that tactics had to be changed to prevent so many BUFFs from being lost. "They [SAC leadership] hated him, but they believed him." Sullivan was commander of Air Force operations at U-Tapao Air Base in Thailand. His direct approach ultimately cost him his career. He retired as a Brigadier.

It was during that night's mission that a friend of Engle's, fellow gunner Jim Cook, was in a B-52 that was hit and lost. Michel describes Cook's experience as the plane exploded while he was trying to bail out: "The explosion had blown Jim Cook clear of the wreckage. 'I woke up on a riverbank in two feet of water, coughing. I had come down headfirst because my legs had been tangled in the chute risers. I hurt all over, and later I found out both legs had been shattered below the knee, my back had been fractured, and my right shoulder and elbow had been broken. The North Vietnamese found me and interrogated me for twenty-four hours, breaking five ribs in the process.'"

Both of Jim Cook's legs were later amputated. Engle remembered Cook visiting his former comrades at Seymour-Johnson AFB in North Carolina: "It was the saddest thing. He visited for a while, and then we didn't see him anymore."

Linebacker Two ended on December 29th. The North Vietnamese ran out of SAMs, and the heavy bombardment over 11 days had worked. Negotiations in Paris were renewed, and on January 27, 1973, the peace agreement was signed by all parties.

Looking back on his part in the bombings, Engle said, "I thought, *Okay, this is really dangerous. If I get killed it's okay. I believe in this.* I would not have traded that for anything. I felt like I was in the right place. I didn't have one question or one doubt. I didn't have any hesitation.

"I think we went into Vietnam for an honorable reason. I believed what was said about communism and still do. I still think we won the war because of the Christmas bombing. We just let it go. I believe we could have had a division like Korea, but there was no more political will."

When Saigon fell in April 1975, Engle was stationed at Seymour-Johnson. He recalled, "I thought it was horrible. I thought we had let them [the South Vietnamese] down."

During his 20-year career, Engle received the Distinguished Flying Cross, the Purple Heart, the Defense Meritorius Service Medal, the Air Force Meritorius Service Medal, and five Air Medals. He flew 100 combat missions over Vietnam.

Classmate **Sharon Jervis** shared her thoughts about the war's end: "I felt sad for all who went."

One of those was her second husband, Sandy Childress, who served two tours in the Army's 1st Air Cav in the Central Highlands of South Vietnam from 1967 to 1969. He graduated in the Class of '66 from a high school in nearby Mt. Vernon. She noted that he suffers from PTSD, and he still has bad dreams. "One of his buddies got killed while next to him," she said.

She noted that "he is gentle as a lamb," and "never talks about Vietnam." In fact, she says that he rarely talks, leaving her feeling somewhat isolated. "I sometimes feel like I'm alone. He doesn't do a lot of talking now."

David Myers concurred that the war had a terrible impact on some veterans. "Some came back all screwed up," he said. And looking back on the war, he added, "We should never have been there. That's obvious."

David Myers '66

David Myers

When he was 20 years old, David was called up to be drafted. However, he was found to have high blood pressure, and was told to try to get it down. He went back twice, and his BP continued to be high. He was finally classified 4-F.

"The Vietnam era was a tragic period in American history," **Arlo Sharp** wrote, "and it permeated my life during my college years and afterwards. It destroyed my confidence and peace of mind, and it sabotaged my choice of career. Of course, that's nothing compared to the loss of nearly 60,000 (American) lives and the thousands of men who returned maimed in body and mind. And the loss of faith in our government.

"Even though U.S. forces won every major engagement and inflicted enormous casualties upon the enemy, everyone lost during the Vietnam era.

"I've often wondered what direction my life would've taken if I'd been accepted by the military. If they had ignored the letter from the orthopedist, perhaps I'd have told them about my anxiety and my suicidal thoughts. But perhaps not, as mental health issues in that era carried a stigma.

"And I'm not sure why I was so terrified of going into the armed forces. Perhaps my mother's worry rubbed off on me. If I'd gone in, I doubt I'd have seen combat. With my education, probably I'd have wound up doing office work somewhere, or teaching children of military personnel. Naturally, I'm no better than anyone else when it comes to risking life and limb for our wonderful country, the greatest nation in history in spite of its mistakes and faults. And I could've enlisted in the armed forces the day after high school graduation and volunteered for the infantry. Perhaps I should've.

"Some say the Vietnam War was necessary to curb the spread of Communism. Without the war, many smaller nations would have been absorbed by the Soviet

Union. Possibly so. History will have to be the judge of that.

"But young men of lower socio-economic status fought the war, shed their blood, and gave their lives. In my high school and town, only that type of guy served. The so-called upper crust, 'in-crowd' youth did not, unless they enlisted and chose to serve.

"As a veteran once observed, 'It's always a rich man's war but a poor man's fight.'

"Returning servicemen were often disrespected and mistreated by the American public. Instead of honor and respect, they were regarded, at best, as second-class citizens and, at worst, as rabid animals. In subtle ways, I saw it happen in my workplace. But I can say with a clear conscience that I always had the greatest respect for them. I was almost one of them."

Sharp ends by saying, "… sometimes I experience survivor's guilt because I'm still alive and a lot of fine young men have been dead for half a century.

"And I'm still not sure why."

CHAPTER FOUR

What Does It Mean To Us?

Through Time: Recalling & Analyzing

The first time I remember hearing anything about Vietnam was when I saw the picture of a Buddhist monk burning himself to death on the streets of Saigon to protest the policies of the South Vietnamese government. The the coup and murder of South Vietnam's president and his brother happened in 1963 during my sophomore year.

I didn't take the matter of war too seriously, though, until the Marines landed at Da Nang in 1965 and it was shown on television. By then, we were high school juniors, and events like that meant that I, or people I knew, could be directly affected.

Edmund Shelby '66

The buildup of U.S. forces continued, and we started talking among ourselves about the war. I remember distinctly being concerned about stepping on a punji stick, and losing a leg.

My brother was a year ahead of me in school, and almost two years older. He was called up for his physical, and our family was worried. He had never been a good student, I believe because of dyslexia, so the prospects of him having to be a ground-pounder were real. What a happy day it was, when he returned and told us he had been rejected because of a knee injury he had sustained in high school.

In my senior year high school yearbook, Jerry Eliott wrote that he would be off to "the University of South Vietnam" while the rest of us would be going to college.

As noted earlier, he did serve there and came safely home.

Indeed some of us did go to college that fall of 1966, and some did well. My good friend Brian Engle and I, however, spent more time with whisky and beer than we did with books. Our college careers lasted one semester.

As that semester was ending, we decided to go downtown in Richmond, Kentucky, to see the Marine recruiter. Fate stepped in, though—the recruiter wasn't there. So we went home to see the local Army recruiter. We knew him, and his son was in our class.

Looking for adventure, we told him we wanted to fly helicopters. He gave us a look of disbelief, and said that he knew our parents, and he wouldn't allow that to happen. He said that helicopter pilots had a lifespan of 15 minutes in Vietnam. He told us to go to the Air Force recruiter, which we did.

We already knew Tech. Sgt. Fannin because he had recruited some of our fellow classmates, such as Elliott, Wyrick, Ratliff and Underwood.

He told us to go to college, but when we explained that we had burned that bridge, he started the paperwork.

After tests and successfully passing our physicals in Louisville, we were signed to go. During this time, since we were no longer in college, the draft board had reclassified us as 1-A.

On May 24, 1967, in the Louisville induction center, we (and 20 or 30 other guys) raised our right hands and swore we would protect the United States and the Constitution against all enemies. Afterward, sitting in the next room, I remember thinking, *What have I gotten myself into?* I wondered where would I go, what would I do, and what would I see in the next four years.

After flying from Louisville to Dallas and from Dallas to San Antonio, I found my world had changed. A loud sergeant informed us that we were no longer home with our mommies, and that we were owned by the United States Air Force. We were loaded on buses, taken first to a chow hall and then to a welcome center. After completing paperwork, we were divided into flights (similar to Army platoons) and taken to our barracks.

The first couple of days weren't all that bad. We received many inoculations, were tested for color-blindness, were given our multiple uniforms, and had all of our hair cut off. This was a time when most young men had fairly long hair—certainly mine was. Brian and I couldn't hold back the laughter when we saw each other.

Then, on day three or four, our drill sergeant showed up. A solid, muscular, yet thin man, Staff Sgt. Turner let us know that the next six weeks were not going to be pleasant. He proved to be correct.

In basic training we were taught how to fire an M-16 rifle, how to make it through a confidence course, how to march as a unit, and how to forget our individuality for the sake of the flight as a whole.

When our time was up, we received our orders for technical training. Mine showed that I was going to Sheppard Air Force Base at Wichita Falls, Texas, to go through Medical Helper school. Brian was also going to Sheppard to learn about computer use.

We got on buses and headed north.

He and I were sent to separate parts of the base, but we agreed that after being settled into our new barracks we would meet at the Airmen's Club. Six weeks is a long time to go without a beer.

Our being new on the base was obvious to the veterans who had been there for a few weeks ahead of us, and they used that opportunity to let us know of their vast superiority by saying "ping." We quickly learned that was supposed to be the sound our hair was making as it started to grow back.

Med Helper was a four-week course that focused on basic medical knowledge, first aid, and disaster response. At the end of that course, we received our orders, which could have been either to an advanced school or to direct duty at a hospital as a "bed pan commando."

My orders said I was to stay at Sheppard to become an operating room technician. That job is now called Surgical Technician, and it consists of scrubbing for surgery to pass instruments to the surgeon and assist when needed. A surgical technician also cleans and sterilizes the instruments and packs for surgery, cleans and disinfects the operating rooms and provides sterile supplies for the rest of the hospital.

The 10-week course lasted until December. I got orders for Fairchild AFB near Spokane, Washington.

Brian and I had said our goodbyes while I was still in training. He was sent to Seymour–Johnson in North Carolina.

Before reporting to Fairchild, I went home and married a girl I had met the previous winter. It wasn't exactly love—maybe we both just wanted something different.

Fairchild was a SAC base. The primary mission for everyone there was to keep the B-52s flying. We at the hospital did that by treating the airmen, their families, and some returnees from Vietnam.

I served there until August 1969. I then was assigned to a hospital in Izmir, Turkey, where I stayed until my discharge in May 1971.

My marriage didn't last. I got a "Dear John" letter while overseas. I didn't want a divorce, but she was adamant, and that was that.

We had a daughter, and my ex-wife wanted me to give her up when she married again. Since my prospects didn't look very good, I agreed. That proved to be one of the great regrets of my life.

I had turned very much against the war while I was in the service. As a result, I was filled with anger when I returned to Corbin. It also didn't help that people I had known all my life didn't want anything to do with me. I guess they saw me as representing all of the bad things about the war. I remember going into a local department store the week I returned. I was with a couple of guys who had also served. The mother of a friend—one I had played with growing up—worked at that store. When she saw me, she turned away. I felt as if I'd been slapped.

I met my present wife while taking some college courses at nearby Cumberland College. She had a young son from a marriage in South Carolina that had not worked out. One of the main reasons for the dissolution of their marriage was because her husband, who had been a Green Beret, came back from Vietnam with a lot of emotional and psychological baggage.

After I graduated from Morehead State University I got my first journalism job, and I adopted her son. One of the best things that ever happened.

Over the years, I have often thought about the Vietnam War and the toll it took on members of my class, the Class of '66. I knew that we were in many ways just a typical small town group that became caught up In something that was much larger. We reacted to it in as many ways as our class of approximately 100 could. Of the guys, many served, some went to and graduated from college, and others did what they could to avoid service.

I believe the leadership of this country never was fully committed to winning the war. If they had been, they would have left the fighting to the generals instead of making tactical decisions in Washington.

Edmund Shelby (left) with Brian Engle

Also, they were cynical about the future of the country after we pulled out. They knew, as noted in Max Hastings' book, that the North Vietnamese would wait a year or two, then advance on the South.

On April 30, 1975, the South surrendered after a lightning advance by Northern troops.

That war directly or indirectly affected these particular people in this typical small Kentucky town. But the war belonged to *everybody* in our generation. For some it was profound. For others it was hardly a blip. But we all remember watching it on television news—and for many young men, there was the threat that we might have to go. Many of us did. Some came back. None were unaffected.

The lasting image most Americans have is of the helicopters on the U.S. Embassy roof in 1975 taking our countrymen and Vietnamese to ships moored offshore in the South China Sea. It's an image of shame—we left many Vietnamese to their fate. And it is an image of terrible waste of men such as Matt Stewart, of billions in money, and of pride in our country.

SOURCES

Vietnam: A History;
    Stanley Karnow;
    Viking Penguin; New York, N.Y.; 1983

Vietnam, An Epic Tragedy, 1945-1975;
    Max Hastings;
    Harper; New York, N.Y.; 2018

Vietnam, A View From The Front Lines;
    Andrew Wiest;
    Osprey; New York, N.Y.; 2013

The Vietnam War Reexamined;
    Michael G. Kort;
    Cambridge University Press;
    Cambridge, U.K.; 2018

Dereliction of Duty;
    H.R. McMaster;
    Harper; New York, N.Y.; 1997

The Road Not Taken;
    Max Boot;
    Liveright Publishing Corp.; New York, N.Y.; 2018

The 11 Days of Christmas, America's Last Vietnam Battle;
    Marshall L. Michel III;
    Encounter Books; New York, N.Y.; 2002

Vietnam: A Complete Photographic History;
    Michael Maclear and Hal Buell;
    Black Dog & Leventhal Publishers;
    New York, N.Y.; 2003

The Mountain Advocate (newspaper);
    Barbourville, KY; 1966

News of the day, lists of popular songs and movies,
    all from Google and *Wikipedia*

Acknowledgments

I want to thank **Scout Larken**
who has helped me through this project
with expertise and care.

Also, I need to thank all the members of the
Corbin High School Class of '66 for their help.
In particular, I must thank
Arlo Sharp and **Brian Engle**,
both of whom contributed so much.

I am particularly grateful to
Lynne Gabbard Keltner,
who put her sharp proofreading skills to good use.

Finally, I must thank
Anne, Graham and **Missy**.

~ES

About the Author

PHOTO: EYE SCOUT IMAGES

EDMUND SHELBY was born and raised in Corbin, Kentucky—in many ways a typically American small town. Growing up, he was influenced by the people of the town and by the news. In fact, he was a newspaper delivery boy. This experience and being on the staff of the high school newspaper led him to choose journalism as a career.

The news of the day informed him of world events, including the happenings in a distant land called

Vietnam. By his senior year in high school, Shelby knew who the major players were in Vietnam, and he'd heard about the buildup of American military forces there.

He and his best friend visited the Marine recruiter's office, but the recruiter was out. They then went to the Army recruiter who told them he knew their parents and was not going to be a part of sending them to Vietnam. He suggested they see the Air Force recruiter, which they did, and they successfully entered the service in May of 1967.

While in the Air Force, Shelby turned against the war. He could see what it was doing to the United States. He did not go to Vietnam, but instead served his overseas duty in Turkey.

Shelby met his wife-to-be and went to college, graduating in 1975, just before the fall of Saigon.

He spent his first three years

as a working journalist in Hazard, Kentucky, before he, his wife and their son moved to Lexington, so she could earn her master's degree from the University of Kentucky. He took a job in public information for state government, working there until the GTE Corporation offered him a better paying position.

In 1992 the family moved to a rural home in Clay County, Kentucky, where he taught at a private school. While teaching, Shelby received the offer of another job in the newspaper business. He practiced journalism for several more years in Beattyville, Jackson and Manchester, Kentucky. During those years, he received numerous awards from the Kentucky Press Association (KPA) and served as president of KPA in 2009.

Shelby, now retired, is still living in Clay County with his wife and their four dogs.

www.ingramcontent.com/pod-product-compliance
Lightning Source LLC
Chambersburg PA
CBHW060331050426
42449CB00011B/2722